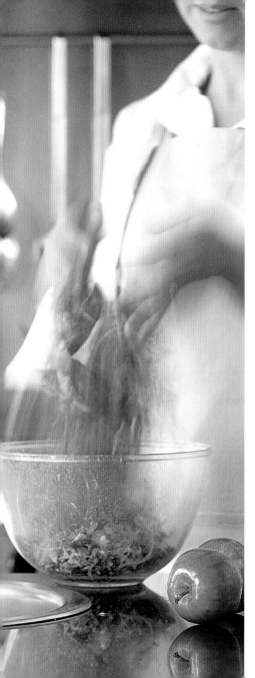

Contents

Elements of a Meal

Cooking and entertaining, like so many other parts of life, are simpler when you have the right tools at hand. The recipes, ideas, and tips presented here are meant as guidelines to help you navigate the way and create your own individual style. Whether preparing a dinner for two, or a celebratory feast for friends, there's much joy to be had in sharing meals together.

Planning a menu

When you're ready to cook a multicourse meal, either for yourselves or for guests, first think about what you feel like eating. And always think seasonally, choosing dishes that make the most of fresh ingredients. Start with one dish or even one ingredient you want to eat, and build a menu from there. Scan the recipes to make sure they work together in terms of time and cooking method. Once you've decided what to serve, make a shopping list, including the tools you'll need.

SEASONAL COOKING

Always consider seasonality when planning a menu. Is it hot midsummer, when lighter fare like salads and cold soups or grilled foods sound good? Or spring, when the markets are overflowing with asparagus and artichokes? Is it chilly autumn or winter, when you want a satisfying stew or roasted meat to warm you up? If you cook with out-of-season ingredients, your food will suffer. Winter tomatoes will be bland and mealy in comparison to the juicy, flavorful tomatoes you remember from last summer.

Following a recipe

The first step is to read each recipe, start to finish. This prevents unpleasant surprises—like discovering one hour before dinnertime that the main dish requires two hours of marinating before it can be grilled! Read the ingredients list and method, and make sure you have everything you need. Unless otherwise noted, ingredients should be at room temperature because they combine better when not too cold. Don't forget to mark down the tools you'll need, and have them on hand so you aren't searching through cupboards in the middle of cooking.

getting organized

Once you have all your ingredients and tools, it's time to set up what chefs call *mise en place* (meez-on-plahs). This French phrase, which translates as "putting in place," means preparing and measuring out your ingredients according to the ingredients list and preparing your equipment according to the recipe method. After this, you're ready to start cooking the meal.

About wine

To many, wine is regarded as food, as indispensable to a fine meal as a good loaf of bread or a leafy green salad. Wine balances the food, aids in digestion, and gives the occasion a convivial feel.

The different shapes of wineglasses are designed to show off the characteristics of the type of wine being served. All wineglasses have a rounded bowl to capture aromas. The more prominent the wine's personality, the bigger the glass.

PAIRING WINE WITH FOOD

While there are tried-and-true combinations of wine and food that seem made for one another, it's ultimately a matter of personal taste, the mood of the moment, or simply what you have on hand. Forget the stiff old rules about pairing reds with meat and whites with fish, and mix and match. Try different combinations of varietals with the same dish, and pay attention to aromas and flavors that please you. The goal is to eat foods you love with wine you love.

About cheese

Many people like to serve cheese with wine when guests first arrive. But some types are so rich and heavy that they easily spoil appetites. As a stylish change of pace, serve a selection of cheeses as a course before dessert or in place of dessert. Plan on two to four types, depending on the number of people you're serving, and aim to offer variety and counterpoint. Or, serve just one cheese, such as a luxurious Camembert or a buttery Gorgonzola, to finish a meal.

ACCOMPANIMENTS TO SERVE WITH CHEESE

Offer a few simple accompaniments with your cheese. Thin slices of baguette or crackers provide a welcome backdrop. Olives and nuts are especially good with goat's milk cheeses. Fruit delivers contrast: classic combinations are crisp apple with Cheddar, and pear with Brie. Dried fruits such as apricots or raisins enhance the flavor of stronger cheeses such as Münster. Pair jams with blue cheese, or honey with hard cheeses like Parmesan.

Entertaining Basics

Sometimes, the need for a party presents itself in an obvious way. Other times, the sense of occasion is more spontaneous. Indeed, often the best excuse for a gathering, be it an afternoon barbecue, a dinner party, or a cocktail fete, may be that there's nothing to celebrate— except the desire to share good food, drink, and fun with friends and family.

Planning the event

Now that you've decided to host a party, give both yourself and your guests time to plan for it. Your party will come off better if you're not rushed when organizing it, and your friends will be more likely to be free if given ample notice of the date: extend invitations at least a week in advance for a casual dinner, or two for a more elaborate affair. After selecting your menu, work together to make a list of what needs to be done and divide up the tasks.

BASIC QUESTIONS

- What type of party do you want to host, and how many guests will you invite?

- What time do you want your guests to arrive, and what time do you imagine them leaving?

- Who will greet them, and where will they put their coats?

- Who will offer them a drink, and what will that drink be?

- What about an appetizer with the drink?

- Do you have enough seating?

Styling the party

It's up to you to create the atmosphere you want at your party. The menu you plan on serving is one key to establishing a mood. And the decorations and tableware you choose, from candles and flowers to glassware and cutlery, will set the scene. Even if you own just one set of white dishes (a versatile choice!), colors and patterns can be brought into your party through table coverings, napkins, flowers and fruit, and serving pieces.

special touches

Your tabletop decor, from the candles to the centerpiece, conveys the spirit of the gathering. Even using simple place cards, laid at each setting, make any dinner party feel special, as do salt and pepper wells. Napkins can be rolled or folded and adorned with a single fresh flower or sprig of herbs. Lighting is yet another way to set the tone. Be kind to your guests and remember that everyone looks good by candlelight. Place tea candles around the table and room, light a fire in the fireplace, or set up tiki torches around the deck to inspire festivity.

A NOTE ON APERITIFS

Offer each guest a refreshment upon arrival. This gesture is both courteous and buys you time for any last-minute preparations. Try the French white aperitif wine Lillet Blanc, served over ice and garnished with an orange twist, or mix Campari with soda or orange juice; these pair well with simple, salty nibbles like olives or nuts. A glass of sparkling wine is a simple and elegant beginning to a party. For a brunch party, add a splash of orange juice to make mimosas, or peach purée to make bellinis.

Setting the table

The arrangements of plates, glasses, and flatware for a place setting may seem arcane and difficult to remember if you don't understand the concept behind it, which is actually quite simple: everything is placed in order of use and within easy reach. For each place setting, lay down the plate, allowing plenty of room between diners. Fold a napkin and place it on the plate, or to the left of the plate and beneath the forks. If you're using a bread plate, position it above the forks.

RULES OF ORDER

Flatware is arranged by order of use from the outside in:

- Forks are set to the left of the plate; salad forks are set to the outside of dinner forks.

- Knives are set to the right of the plate with blade facing the plate.

- Spoons are set to the outside of the knife when soup is on the menu.

Glasses sit above the knife. Wineglasses sit to the right of water glasses, in the order in which they will be served.

TIPS FOR HOSTS

● Get organized. The more elaborate the party, the more organized you need to be. Make checklists and timelines. Don't leave all of the shopping and food preparation until the last minute: do each task as far in advance as it can be done. Determine what dishes or chores can be completed ahead of time, and how far ahead.

● Well in advance of the party, make sure you have all the required cooking equipment and serving utensils.

● Work as a team. Plot everything out on paper, then divide up the tasks in a way that works for you as a couple.

● Practice makes perfect. Even if you are an experienced cook, don't try out a recipe for the first time on the day of the party. A trial run will make cooking for your guests go more smoothly, and will allow you to make any adjustments to the menu.

● Do yourself a favor and plan your first dinner parties for Saturday nights. This gives you an entire day for last-minute shopping, decorating, and cooking—and another entire day to recover, rest, and clean up! Save the more stressful weeknight dinner parties for when you feel more experienced and confident, or very organized.

Creating a home bar

The ritual and ceremony involved in cocktail construction are probably as much fun as drinking the cocktail itself, and the bar area is where guests are most likely to congregate. So, take some time to carefully plan the space. If you don't have a stand-alone or built-in bar, you can create a temporary or permanent one using a cabinet, bookshelf, cart, or side table. Since guests will be milling around the bar, try to pick a spot that won't interfere with the flow of traffic throughout the rooms.

stocking your home bar

Stocking the bar may seem overwhelming (and rather expensive) unless you buy supplies incrementally, tailored to your favorite drinks and the preferences of friends. Use the list at right as a starting point and gradually fill it in with your own preferred spirits, liqueurs, mixers, and wines and beers. Always keep plenty of soda and sparkling fruit juices for guests who won't be drinking alcohol, as well as garnishes like lemon and lime wedges, olives, and maraschino cherries.

COCKTAIL PARTY TIPS

● Plan on serving three drinks per every two hours for each guest. This may seem like a lot, but it is better to have extra on hand than to come up short.

● Be sure to stock up on plenty of ice for mixed drinks. Place an ice bucket with tongs on the bar and replenish it regularly.

● As responsible hosts, you will want to provide your guests with sufficient food and water to prevent drunkenness, and hot coffee as the evening winds down.

THE BASIC BAR

— VODKA AND/OR GIN

— SILVER TEQUILA

— RUM, LIGHT AND DARK

— SCOTCH WHISKY

— BOURBON

— DRY (WHITE) VERMOUTH

— ANGOSTURA BITTERS

— TRIPLE SEC OR COINTREAU

— BRANDY AND/OR COGNAC

— SODA AND TONIC; FRUIT JUICES

Dinner Party

Celery Root Soup

Fennel Salad with Blood Oranges,
Arugula, and Shaved Parmesan

Pork Loin with Sweet Mustard Glaze

Spiced Fig and Honey Clafoutis

White-wine pairing: **off-dry Riesling**
Red-wine pairing: **Pinot Noir**
Dessert-wine pairing: **orange Muscat or tawny Port**

SERVES 6–8

Food and drink tips

- **Serve salty nibbles:**
With cocktails, offer your
guests a simple appetizer,
such as an antipasti plate
of Italian meats and
cheeses; almond-stuffed
olives; figs wrapped with
prosciutto; or radishes
with sea salt and butter.

- **Stock up on beverages:**
Have plenty of drinks on
hand, including wine, beer,
sparkling water, and juice.
You might want to start
off the evening with a
special cocktail.

- **Serve family style:**
Present this meal on
platters for a convivial
mood at the table and less
work for you ferrying plates
from the kitchen.

- **Post-meal coffee:**
Early in the day, set up
coffee and tea service so
you won't have to worry
about it during dinner.

General party tips

- **Keep the lighting soft:**
Candles add a warm glow to any table or party and are far more flattering than overhead or direct lighting.

- **Set up early:**
Arrange flowers and any other decorations around the dining area and set the table well before party time.

- **Select music:**
For a stylish choice, try a classic jazz album like John Coltrane's *Blue Train* or Miles Davis's *Kind of Blue*.

- **As guests arrive:**
One spouse takes coats while the other offers drinks and appetizers.

Celery Root Soup

preparation **30** minutes | cooking **1½** hours | **6–8** first-course servings

tools | chef's knife | vegetable peeler | large saucepan | wooden spatula | blender | ladle
optional tools | whisk | colander | tongs

Melt the butter over medium-low heat in a large saucepan. Add the onion, leek, and thyme sprig and cook gently, stirring often, until the onion and leek are translucent but not browned, about 5 minutes. Add the celery root, partially cover the pan, and cook for 10 minutes. Check occasionally and add a few tablespoons of water if the celery root begins to brown. Add the wine, adjust the heat so that the liquid simmers briskly, and cook until reduced by half, about 20 minutes. Add the stock, partially cover the pan, and let simmer until the celery root is very tender, about 45 minutes. Remove from the heat and let cool, uncovered, for about 5 minutes.

Remove the thyme sprig and, working in batches if necessary, purée the soup in a blender or food processor or with a stick blender until completely smooth. (If using a stand blender, be sure to hold the top on firmly when blending hot liquids.) Return to the pan and stir in the salt and a generous pinch of pepper. Taste and adjust the seasoning. *At this point, the soup can be held for up to 1½ hours.*

When ready to serve, reheat the soup gently over medium heat, stirring occasionally, if needed. Ladle into bowls. Garnish with the sautéed shallots and thyme leaves, if using, and serve hot.

3 Tbsp unsalted butter

1 large yellow onion, finely chopped

1 leek, white part only, well washed and finely chopped

1 large sprig fresh thyme, plus leaves for garnish (optional)

1 lb (500 g) celery root (celeriac), peeled and coarsely chopped

2 cups (16 fl oz/500 ml) dry white wine

3 cups (24 fl oz/750 ml) vegetable stock

¾ tsp fine sea salt

Freshly ground white pepper

Lightly sautéed shallots for garnish (optional)

Fennel Salad with Blood Oranges, Arugula, and Shaved Parmesan

preparation **20** minutes | **6–8** servings

tools | chef's knife | salad spinner | large mixing bowl | whisk | vegetable peeler

2 bulbs fennel, stems and fronds removed

4 blood or navel oranges

6 Tbsp (3 fl oz/90 ml) extra-virgin olive oil

2 Tbsp red wine vinegar

¼ tsp fine sea salt

¼ tsp freshly ground pepper

4 cups (4 oz/125 g) loosely packed arugula (rocket) leaves, spun dry

2-oz (60-g) chunk Parmesan cheese

Remove any bruised outer leaves from the fennel bulbs and trim off any discolored bits. Cut a slice off the top and bottom of each orange. Working with 1 orange at a time, stand it on a cut side and carefully slice off the peel and white pith to expose the flesh, following the curve of the fruit with the knife. *At this point, the trimmed fennel and oranges can be held for up to 3 hours.*

Quarter the fennel bulbs, cut out the tough cores, and thinly slice them lengthwise. Slice the oranges crosswise into thin rounds and remove the seeds. *At this point, the sliced fennel and oranges can be held for up to 20 minutes.*

In a large bowl, whisk together the olive oil, vinegar, salt, and pepper. Add the arugula and fennel and toss to coat evenly with the vinaigrette. Mound on a platter and distribute the orange slices over and around the salad. Using a vegetable peeler, shave the Parmesan over the salad in thin curls. Serve the salad as soon as possible; refrigerate if it will be held for more than 10 minutes.

Pork Loin with Sweet Mustard Glaze

preparation **10** minutes | standing **30** minutes | cooking **1** hour **25** minutes |
resting **10** minutes | **6–8** servings

tools | chef's knife | citrus reamer | small mixing bowl | whisk | small saucepan | roasting pan |
roasting rack | brush | instant-read thermometer

Pat the pork roast dry with paper towels. Let stand at room
temperature for 30 minutes–1 hour before roasting. Preheat
the oven to 400°F (200°C).

To make the glaze, whisk together the ginger preserves,
shallot, lemon juice, olive oil, and mustard in a small bowl.
Pour half of the glaze into a small saucepan.

Line a roasting pan with foil. Place the roast, fat side up, on
a rack in the roasting pan. Brush generously on all sides with
some of the glaze from the bowl and season with salt and
pepper. Roast the pork for 25 minutes, then reduce the oven
temperature to 325°F (165°C) and roast for about 1 hour
longer, basting occasionally with the glaze from the bowl.
When an instant-read thermometer inserted into the thickest
part registers 145°F (63°C), the roast is done. Remove from
the oven and let the pork rest on the rack, loosely covered
with foil, for 10 minutes.

While the pork is resting, place the glaze in the saucepan
over medium heat and bring to a simmer to warm, then remove
from the heat. Transfer the roast to a cutting board. Using a
sharp knife, cut the pork into slices ½ inch (12 mm) thick.
Serve the pork with a generous drizzle of the warmed glaze,
garnished with sage, if using.

One 4-lb (2-kg) boneless
center-cut pork loin
roast, about 3½ inches
(9 cm) in diameter

FOR THE GLAZE

⅔ cup (6½ oz/200 g)
ginger preserves

½ cup (2½ oz/75 g)
minced shallot

½ cup (4 fl oz/125 ml)
fresh lemon juice

⅓ cup (3 fl oz/80 ml)
extra-virgin olive oil

⅓ cup (3 oz/90 g) Dijon
mustard

Fine sea salt and freshly
ground pepper

Fresh sage leaves for
garnish (optional)

Spiced Fig and Honey Clafoutis

standing **45** minutes | preparation **20** minutes | cooking **35** minutes | **6–8** servings

tools | chef's knife | box grater | small saucepan | small mixing bowl | oval baking dish | large mixing bowl | whisk | slotted spoon | fine-mesh sieve

¼ cup (3 fl oz/80 ml) honey

1 lb (500 g) dried figs (about 2½ cups), halved lengthwise

2 large eggs plus 1 large egg yolk

⅔ cup (3 oz/90 g) granulated sugar

¼ cup (1½ oz/45 g) all-purpose (plain) flour

¼ tsp freshly grated nutmeg

¼ tsp ground allspice

¼ tsp ground cinnamon

1¼ cups (10 fl oz/310 ml) heavy (double) cream

4 Tbsp (2 oz/60 g) unsalted butter, melted

⅓ cup (1½ oz/45 g) coarsely chopped walnuts (optional)

Powdered (icing) sugar for dusting

In a small bowl, dissolve the honey in 1 cup (8 fl oz/ 250 ml) very hot water and add the figs. Toss and let stand for 45 minutes to plump the fruit, tossing occasionally.

Preheat the oven to 400°F (200°C). Butter the bottom and sides of a 12-inch (30-cm) oval or similar-sized baking dish. Sprinkle with granulated sugar and tap to shake out the excess.

In a large mixing bowl, whisk together the eggs and egg yolk, then whisk in the granulated sugar. Add the flour, nutmeg, allspice, and cinnamon and stir to combine, then stir in the cream and melted butter until well blended.

Using a slotted spoon, transfer the figs to the baking dish, spreading them evenly. Whisk the honey liquid remaining in the bowl into the egg batter. Scatter the walnuts over the figs, if using, and pour the batter evenly over the top. Bake until puffy and golden, about 35 minutes. Serve warm, using a fine-mesh sieve to dust each serving with a little powdered sugar.

Techniques

Dicing onions

1 Halve the onion
Using a chef's knife, cut the onion in half lengthwise through the root end. This makes it easier to peel and creates a flat side.

2 Cut lengthwise
Hold the onion half securely. With the knife, make a series of lengthwise cuts as thick as you want the final dice to be.

3 Cut horizontally
Turn the blade parallel to the cutting board and make a series of horizontal cuts as thick as you want the final dice to be.

4 Cut crosswise
Holding the half with your fingers, cut it crosswise into dice. To mince the pieces, rock the blade back and forth.

Mincing shallots

1 Peel & cut the shallot
Make a series of thin lengthwise cuts then turn the knife blade parallel to the cutting board and make a series of horizontal cuts.

2 Cut crosswise
Cut the shallot half crosswise to make dice. Dicing a shallot in this methodical way yields pieces that will cook evenly.

Working with leeks

1 Trim the leeks

Using a chef's knife, trim off the roots and tough dark green tops of the leeks, leaving only the white and pale green parts.

2 Halve & quarter

Cut each leek in half lengthwise. Place each half, cut side down on a cutting board, and cut it in half again to create quarters.

3 Rinse

Holding the root ends, and separating the layers to expose any dirt, swish the leeks in a bowl of cold water.

4 Cut crosswise

Pat the leeks dry. Using a chef's knife, and holding the layers of the quarter together, cut each leek crosswise into slices.

Mincing garlic

1 Halve & slice the garlic

Peel and halve each garlic clove. One at a time, use the knife to cut the garlic clove halves into very thin slices. Use as is or chop.

2 Mince

Gather the chopped garlic in a pile. Continue to chop, rocking the blade back and forth, until the garlic pieces are very fine.

Techniques

Sectioning citrus

1 Cut away peel & pith

Slice off the top and bottom of the fruit and stand on a flat end. Following the fruit's curve, cut away all the peel and white pith.

2 Release segments

Working over a bowl, make a cut on both sides of each segment to free it from the membrane, letting it drop into the bowl.

Making a basic vinaigrette

1 Whisk vinegar & salt

In a medium bowl, whisk together 3 Tbsp vinegar and ¼ tsp salt until the salt begins to dissolve.

2 Whisk in mustard

Whisk ½ tsp mustard into the vinegar-salt mixture to add flavor and act as an emulsifier to stabilize the oil and vinegar.

3 Slowly add oil

Gradually add ¾ cup (6 fl oz/ 180 ml) extra-virgin olive oil while whisking rapidly in a circular motion.

4 Use or store

Whisk in ⅛ tsp freshly ground pepper. Use the vinaigrette right away, or store it for up to 5 days in a jar or other glass container.

Separating eggs

1 Pull shells apart

Hold a cracked egg over an empty bowl and carefully pull the shell apart, letting the white start to drop into the bowl.

2 Pass yolk back & forth

Transfer the yolk back and forth from one shell half to the other, letting the remaining egg white fall into the bowl below.

3 Separate yolk

Gently drop the yolk into a second bowl. Keeping the whites free of any yolk is key if you plan to whip the whites.

4 Transfer whites

If the egg separates cleanly, pour the white into a third bowl. Break each new egg over the first empty bowl and transfer.

Whipping egg whites

1 Beat egg whites

Using a mixer, beat room-temperature whites with a pinch of cream of tartar on medium speed until foamy, 1 minute.

2 Look for peaks

Soft peaks: beat on medium-high speed until opaque, 2–3 minutes; stiff peaks: beat 1–2 minutes longer, until glossy.

Tools

Cook's tools

Chef's knife

With its large, tapered, evenly proportioned blade, this knife is used for a variety of kitchen tasks, including slicing and chopping.

Peelers

The best models come with blades that swivel, to adjust to the contours of whatever you are peeling.

Box grater

Made of stainless steel, this kitchen standby presents you with a choice of different cutting surfaces, typically four to six.

Salad spinner

A spinner quickly dries rinsed salad greens or other leafy items through rapid rotation; excess water is spun off into the bowl.

Mixing bowls

Nesting bowls are indispensable for tasks like holding small measured amounts of ingredients and mixing cake batters.

Instant-read thermometer

A thermometer enables you to determine at a glance the precise degree of doneness for meat, poultry, or fish as it cooks.

Cookware and bakeware

Basting brushes

These make it easy to soak up pan juices, marinades, or glazes and apply them to the surface of meat as it cooks.

Saucepan

This simple round pan has either straight or slightly sloping sides and generally ranges in size from 1–5 quarts (1–5 liters).

Roasting pan

This large, rectangular pan has low sides to allow the oven's heat to reach as much of the food as possible during roasting.

Handheld strainers

Made of wire mesh, these strainers come in a range of sizes and are useful for sifting and a multitude of other kitchen tasks.

Roasting rack

Placed inside a roasting pan to support a large piece of meat or a whole bird, this rack allows more of the food to brown.

Baking dishes

Used for baking savory main courses, casseroles, or desserts, these deep, ovenproof dishes come in a variety of shapes.

Barbecue Party

Grilled Corn and Tomato Salad

Dry-Rubbed Ribs

Jicama Slaw with Chile-Lime Dressing

Buttermilk Corn Bread

Citrus-Scented Grapes and Melon

Beer pairing: Belgian ale
Red-wine pairing: chilled Beaujolais nouveau

SERVES 8–10

Food and drink tips

- **Pick grill-friendly drinks:** Choose a range of beers, from artisanal Belgian ales to flavorful microbrews. For wine, provide a crisp Sauvignon Blanc for white and a young red, such as Beaujolais nouveau. Round out your beverage choices with some homemade iced tea garnished with mint.

- **Provide salty snacks:** Place bowls of nuts, pretzels, or potato chips and creamy dip on outdoor tables.

- **Prepare the meal ahead:** Make the dry rub for the ribs up to a week ahead of time; the day before, cut meat slabs into individual ribs and season with rub; grill corn and refrigerate, and make syrup for fruit.

General barbecue tips

- **Self-serve drinks:**
Fill galvanized tubs with
ice, put out bottle openers
and glasses, and let guests
choose their own drinks;
place snacks nearby.

- **Keep it casual:**
Set one long table and
pass platters of food for
a family-style meal, or set
up a buffet for guests.

- **Make it fun:**
Hang a piñata for guests
to whack at or set up
bocce, boules, or croquet
to encourage mingling
and playing.

- **Use outdoor cutlery:**
For alfresco dining, use
wood or bamboo cutlery;
bundle each set in a napkin
tied with a colorful ribbon.

Grilled Corn and Tomato Salad

preparation **45** minutes | cooking **20** minutes | **8–10** side-dish servings

tools | small saucepan | chef's knife | citrus reamer | kitchen shears | serrated utility knife | small mixing bowl | whisk | brush | grill or grill pan | wire grill brush (optional) | tongs

In a small bowl, whisk together the melted butter, Tabasco, basil, ½ tsp of the salt, and ¼ tsp of the black pepper. Place 3 sheets of foil each 15 inches (38 cm) long on a work surface, and place 2 ears of corn on each sheet. Brush the corn with the butter mixture. Wrap up snugly.

Prepare a fire in a charcoal grill or preheat a gas grill to medium. Scrape the rack clean with a wire brush, if necessary, and use paper towels to brush it lightly with olive oil. Position the grill rack or broiler pan about 4 inches (10 cm) from the heat source. (Alternatively, preheat a well-seasoned ridged stove-top grill pan.) Grill the corn packages for 10 minutes, turning occasionally with tongs. Unwrap the corn and grill the ears directly on the grill rack (or pan) for 5–10 minutes longer, turning to brown each side evenly. Watch the corn carefully; it should be nicely charred but not blackened.

When the corn is cool enough to handle, place each ear over a large serving bowl and cut off the kernels, keeping the blade angled so you get the whole kernel but none of the tough cob. Add the lime juice, ½ cup (4 fl oz / 125 ml) olive oil, the chives, the remaining ½ tsp salt, and the remaining ¼ tsp black pepper to the bowl with the corn and toss to combine. Add the watercress and cherry tomatoes and toss gently. Serve at once.

6 Tbsp (3 oz/90 g) unsalted butter, melted

3 drops of Tabasco sauce or pinch of ground cayenne pepper

2 Tbsp finely chopped fresh basil

1 tsp fine sea salt

½ tsp freshly ground black pepper

6 ears white or yellow corn, husks and silks removed

Extra-virgin olive oil for brushing, plus ½ cup (4 fl oz/125 ml)

2 Tbsp fresh lime juice

2 Tbsp finely snipped fresh chives

1 bunch watercress, tough stems removed, separated into small sprigs

4 cups (24 oz/750 g) cherry tomatoes, halved through the stem end

Dry-Rubbed Ribs

preparation **10** minutes | marinating **2** hours | cooking **2¼** hours | **8–10** servings

tools | very large mixing bowl | large lock-top plastic bags | 2 large roasting pans | grill (optional) | wire grill brush (optional) | tongs

FOR THE DRY RUB

⅔ cup (2 oz/60 g) paprika

¼ cup (½ oz/15 g) freshly ground black pepper

¼ cup (2 oz/60 g) firmly packed dark brown sugar

3 Tbsp fine sea salt

4 tsp celery salt

4 tsp garlic powder

4 tsp dry mustard

4 tsp ground cumin

1½ tsp ground cayenne pepper

10 lb (5 kg) spareribs (about 35 ribs when individually cut)

Vegetable oil for grill (optional)

In a very large bowl, stir together all the dry rub ingredients until thoroughly blended. *At this point, the rub can be stored at room temperature for up to 1 week in an airtight container.*

Add the ribs to the bowl of rub 5 at a time and rub the spices into them evenly on all sides. Transfer the ribs to large lock-top plastic bags, about 5 to a bag, letting the excess rub fall back into the bowl. Reserve excess rub for later use. *Let stand at room temperature for at least 2 hours, or refrigerate for up to overnight. Return to room temperature before cooking.*

Preheat the oven to 325°F (165°C). Divide the ribs between 2 very large roasting pans, placing them fatty side up. Bake until the meat is golden brown and no longer pink at the bone, 1½–1¾ hours. *At this point, the ribs can stand at room temperature for up to 1 hour before finishing on the grill.*

Prepare a fire in a charcoal grill, preheat a gas grill to medium-high, or preheat the broiler (grill). If using a charcoal or gas grill, scrape the rack clean with a wire brush, if necessary, and use paper towels to brush it lightly with oil. Position the grill rack or broiler pan about 4 inches (10 cm) from the heat source.

Sprinkle any remaining rub mixture over the cooked ribs and brown briefly on the grill or under the broiler until sizzling. The ribs may be served hot or warm.

Jicama Slaw with Chile-Lime Dressing

preparation **25** minutes | chilling **1** hour | **8–10** side-dish servings

tools | citrus reamer | salad spinner (optional) | chef's knife | vegetable peeler | box grater | large mixing bowl | whisk | 2 wooden spoons

1½ lb (750 g) jicama

¾ lb (375 g) carrots

1 cup (1 oz/30 g) loosely packed fresh cilantro (fresh coriander) leaves

1 jalapeño chile

¼ cup (2 fl oz/60 ml) fresh lime juice

¼ cup (2 oz/60 g) sour cream

¼ cup (2 fl oz/60 ml) mayonnaise, homemade if desired

1 tsp fine sea salt

½ tsp chile powder

Pale inner leaves from 1 large head romaine (cos) lettuce (8–10 leaves), spun dry (optional)

With a vegetable peeler, peel the jicama and the carrots. Use the largest holes of a box grater to coarsely shred both. You should have about 4 cups firmly packed shredded jicama and 2 cups carrots.

Finely chop the cilantro leaves. Halve, seed, and mince the chile.

In a large glass or ceramic bowl, combine the lime juice, sour cream, mayonnaise, salt, chile powder, jalapeño, and cilantro and whisk together. Add the jicama and carrots and toss to mix. Cover and refrigerate for at least 1 hour to allow the flavors to blend.

Remove the salad from the refrigerator just before serving. Toss again to distribute the dressing. Scoop some salad into each lettuce leaf, if using, and serve.

Buttermilk Corn Bread

preparation **30** minutes | cooking **15** minutes | cooling **10** minutes | **8–10** side-dish servings

tools | small saucepan | chef's knife | muffin pan | large mixing bowl | whisk | cooling rack

Preheat the oven to 425°F (220°C). Butter a standard 12-cup muffin pan or a 3-qt (3-l) baking dish.

In a large bowl, stir together the cornmeal, flour, sugar, baking powder, 1 tsp salt, and ½ tsp pepper. Make a well in the center of the mixture and add the egg, buttermilk, melted butter, corn, and cayenne. Using a fork to whisk from the center, blend the ingredients into a lumpy batter; do not overmix.

Pour the batter into the prepared muffin cups or dish and bake until lightly browned and pulling away from the sides of the pan, about 15 minutes for a muffin pan, 25 minutes for a baking dish. Transfer to a wire rack and let cool for about 10 minutes. Turn the muffins or bread out of the pan or dish. Serve warm or at room temperature.

1 cup (6 oz/185 g) cornmeal

1 cup (5 oz/155 g) all-purpose (plain) flour

2 Tbsp sugar

2 tsp baking powder

Fine sea salt and black pepper

1 large egg, lightly beaten

1 cup (8 fl oz/250 ml) buttermilk

6 Tbsp (3 oz/90 g) unsalted butter, melted

1 cup (6 oz/185 g) corn kernels

⅛ tsp ground cayenne pepper

Citrus-Scented Grapes and Melon

preparation **30** minutes | cooking **10** minutes | chilling **2** hours | **8–10** dessert servings

tools | citrus reamer | chef's knife | small saucepan | mixing bowl | vegetable peeler | sieve | medium saucepan | heatproof bowl

1 lemon

1 cup (8 oz/250 g) sugar

4 Tbsp fresh lemon juice

½ tsp orange flower water

1 large cantaloupe, about 3½ lb (1.75 kg), halved and seeded

12 oz (375 g) seedless green grapes, halved

¾ cup (3 oz/90 g) unsalted pistachio nuts, coarsely chopped

Orange zest strips for garnish (optional)

Bring a small saucepan of water to a boil. Have ready a bowl of ice water. Cut the zest from the lemon in wide strips and then cut into matchstick-sized strips. When the water comes to a boil, add the zest and blanch for 1 minute. Scoop up the zest with a sieve and place it in the ice water to stop the cooking. Drain the zest.

Combine 1¼ cups (10 fl oz/310 ml) water, the sugar, and the lemon juice in a medium saucepan. Place over low heat, cover, and heat, swirling the pan occasionally, until the sugar dissolves. Uncover the pan, raise the heat to medium-high, and bring to a boil. Add the blanched lemon zest and adjust the heat to achieve a gentle simmer. Cook until the syrup is very slightly thickened, about 7 minutes. Pour the syrup into a heatproof bowl, stir in the orange flower water, and set aside to cool to room temperature. Cover and refrigerate until well chilled, at least 2 hours. *At this point, the syrup may be refrigerated for up to 2 days.*

Slice the melon, cut off the rind, and cut the flesh into ¾-inch (2-cm) cubes. In a serving bowl, combine the melon and grapes. Pour the chilled syrup over the fruit and toss gently to coat. Scatter with the pistachios and orange zest strips, if using, and serve.

Techniques

Shredding carrots

1 Trim carrots

Use a vegetable peeler to peel the skin from the carrots, then use a chef's knife to trim off the leafy tops and rootlike ends.

2 Peel & grate

Using the vegetable peeler or the largest holes of a box grater, peel or grate the carrots into long, thin strips.

Dicing tomatoes

1 Cut vertical slices

Make a shallow circular cut to remove the cores. Place each half cut side down and make a series of thin slices.

3 Cut into dice

Line up the strips and cut crosswise into small dice; push aside. Repeat steps 1–3 with the remaining tomato halves.

2 Cut into strips

Stack 2 or 3 of the tomato slices at a time on their sides. Make a second series of thin slices, perpendicular to the first.

4 Transfer the dice

Use the flat side of a chef's knife to scoop up the pieces and transfer the diced tomatoes from the board to a prep bowl.

Working with fresh herbs

Mincing citrus zest

1 Select the herb

Large- and small-leafed herbs like basil and thyme are easy to sliver, chop, or mince; cilantro and tarragon are more delicate.

2 Remove the leaves

Rinse the herbs and pat them dry. Use your fingers to pull off the leaves. Discard the stems and any discolored leaves.

1 Remove the zest

Use a vegetable peeler to remove strips of just the colored portion of the peel, not the bitter white pith.

3 Chop the leaves

Gather the leaves in a pile. Rest your fingertips on the tip of a chef's knife and rock the blade back and forth to chop coarsely.

4 Mince the leaves

Continue to regather the leaves and rock the blade over them until they are chopped into very fine pieces (minced).

2 Cut & mince the zest

Stack 2 or 3 zest strips, then use a chef's knife to cut them lengthwise into very thin strips. Cut crosswise into fine pieces.

Techniques

Juicing citrus

1 Halve the fruit

Press and roll the fruit firmly against the work surface to loosen membranes. Using a chef's knife, cut in half crosswise.

2 Juice the citrus

Use a citrus reamer to pierce the membranes as you turn and squeeze the fruit. You can also use a citrus press or juicer.

Working with chiles

1 Quarter lengthwise

Using a paring knife, cut the chile into halves, then into quarters; wear latex gloves, if desired, to prevent irritation.

2 Remove seeds & ribs

Using the paring knife, cut away the seeds and ribs from each chile quarter; removing these lessens the heat.

3 Slice into strips

Place the quarters, cut side up, on the cutting board. Cut into narrow strips about ⅛ inch (3 mm) wide.

4 Dice and mince

Line up the chile strips and cut them crosswise at thin intervals. Rock the blade back and forth over the pieces to mince them.

Direct heat

1 Pour ignited coals

When the coals in the chimney starter are covered with white ash, use a grill mitt to dump them into the fire bed.

2 Arrange coals

Using long-handled tongs, arrange the coals 2 or 3 layers deep in two-thirds of fire bed to form heat zones.

Indirect heat

1 Arrange coals

Pour coals into the firebed, then use long-handled tongs to arrange the coals in 2 equal piles on 2 sides of the grill.

2 Add drip pan

Place an aluminum-foil pan in the center to catch the dripping fat and create a cool zone. Add water to fill pan halfway.

Oiling a grill

1 Dip rolled towels in oil

Fold a few paper towels in half, then roll them up into a cylinder. Using tongs, soak the towels in a container with some canola oil.

2 Brush the grate

Using the tongs, brush the grill grate with the oiled towels. This keeps food from sticking to the grill and makes cleanup easier.

Tools

Grilling tools

Grill

The two most popular types of outdoor grills are the propane- or natural gas-fueled gas grill, and the kettle-type charcoal grill.

Vegetable basket

This hinged wire grid, which comes in a range of sizes and shapes, is used to grill small vegetables such as asparagus.

Grill pan

A cast-iron or anodized aluminum skillet or griddle with ridges across the bottom that deliver nicely browned marks.

Wire grill brush

The best tool for cleaning a grill is a stiff, rustproof wire brush, which can be used before or after cooking to remove residue.

Long-handled tool set

Extra-long, heatproof handles make these suitable for working with the intense heat of the grill and cumbersome items.

Muffin pan

Standard muffin pans have 6 or 12 cups that each hold about 6 tablespoons (3 fl oz/90 ml) of batter; other sizes are available.

Cook's tools

Serrated knife

The sharp serrated edge of this long, straight blade cuts easily through the tough crusts and tender interiors of bread loaves.

Kitchen shears

These heavy-duty clippers are handy for cutting up fruit, flowers, and even sheets of parchment (baking) paper.

Wooden spoons

Indispensable in the kitchen, wooden spoons are sturdy, do not scratch bowls or pans, and stay cool to the touch.

Citrus reamer

Press and twist citrus halves against the ridged, mound-shaped surface of this tool to squeeze juice.

Tongs

These hinged tools with blunt ends are useful for gently picking up pieces of food, tossing salads, and other jobs.

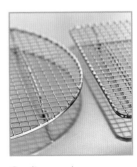

Cooling rack

Wire racks with feet allow air to circulate and prevent moisture from being trapped under baked goods.

—— WILLIAMS-SONOMA ——
WEDDING & GIFT REGISTRY

Congratulations—and thank you for registering at Williams-Sonoma. We hope that this book will help you cook and entertain happily ever after.

More recipes and tips can be found in the following books:

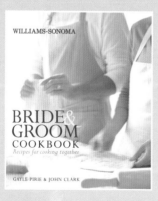
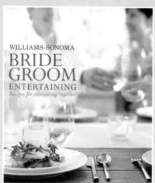

WELDON OWEN

Content from Williams-Sonoma *Bride and Groom Cookbook*, *Bride and Groom Entertaining*, and *Tools & Techniques*.

Copyright © 2009 Weldon Owen Inc. and Williams-Sonoma Inc.

ISBN 13: 978-1-74089-881-2

Printed in China